1 Read. Then match.

1 What does she look like?

   a She is intelligent and kind.

   b She is Chinese.

   c She has got blue eyes.

2 Is he tall?

   a Yes, he has.

   b Yes, he is.

   c No, he hasn't got it.

3 What do they look like?

   a They are looking at the teacher.

   b They like watching TV.

   c They are handsome.

4 What do you look like?

   a I'm looking at a book.

   b I've got brown hair and blue eyes.

   c I like ice cream.

2 Order to make questions. Then match.

1 look / what / she / like / does

   <u>What does she look like?</u>

   a He's small and thin.

2 tall / they / handsome / are / and

   _____ ?

   b No, he hasn't.

3 he / has / blue / eyes / got

   _____ ?

   c Yes, they are.

4 do / look / what / like / they

   _____ ?

   d They are tall and thin.

5 does / he / like / what / look

   _____ ?

   e She's got long straight hair.

3 Read. Then answer the questions.

1 What's he like?

<u>He's clever and kind.</u> _____ (clever / kind)

2 What's she like?

_____ . (talkative / helpful)

3 What are they like?

_____ . (hard-working / shy)

4 What's he like?

_____ . (friendly / but / bossy)

5 What are you like?

_____ ! (sporty / clever)

4 Look at the picture. What does he/she look like? What is he/she like? Write.

He's / She's _____ .

He's / She's got _____ .

I like him / her because he's / she's _____

_____ .

5 Complete the sentences using the *comparative / superlative*.

Name	Age	Height
Tom	9 years 3 months	1.26 metres
Julia	9 years 6 months	1.2 metres
Steve	9 years 1 month	1.21 metres
Anita	8 years 10 months	1.22 metres

1 Tom is _taller_ than Julia. He is the _____ in the group.

2 Anita is _____ but _____ than Julia.

3 Julia is _____ than Tom . She is the _____ in the group.

4 Anita and Steve _____ .

5 Julia and Tom _____ .

6 Complete the sentences.

1 Mount Everest is _the highest_ mountain in the world. (high)

2 The Pacific Ocean is _____ ocean in the world. (deep)

3 The lion is _____ the giraffe. (fast)

4 China is _____ Spain. (big)

5 The Nile is _____ river in the world. (long)

7 Look at the pictures. Then write sentences using the *comparative / superlative*.

a  b  c

small intelligent bored excited ~~important~~ lovely

d  e  f

1 _Picture b is the most important._ .

2 _____ .

3 _____ .

4 _____ .

5 _____ .

6 _____ .

8 **Order to make sentences.**

1 is / friend / my / Tom / best

_____ .

2 hair / blue / he / spiky / short / eyes / got / and / has

_____ .

3 taller / me / than / he / is / I / that / think

_____ .

4 intelligent / he / more / is / me / than

_____ .

5 cleverest / boy / class / he / is / the / our / in

_____ .

6 grandad / the / person / my / is / in / family / oldest / my

_____ .

7 Tom / lazy / my / at / friend / home / school / but / at / is / hard-working

_____ .

9 **Complete the sentences.**

1 Sara is _____ me. (short)

2 She is _____ person in our class. (short)

3 She's got long brown hair.

She's got _____ hair in our class. (long)

4 She is very kind but a bit bossy.

She is _____ me. (bossy)

5 I think she is _____ person in our class. (bossy)

6 She is hard-working, but I think I am _____ than she is. (hard-working)

7 But she is _____ me. (intelligent)

1 **Read. Then match.**

I'm bored!

1	I'm hungry.	**a**	You should look under your bed!
2	I'm cold.	**b**	You should listen to the instructions!
3	I'm bored.	**c**	You should eat something.
4	I'm tired.	**d**	You should put on your coat.
5	I don't know what to do.	**e**	You should meet your friends.
6	I can't find my mobile.	**f**	You shouldn't watch TV so late.

2 **Order to make sentences.**

1 remember / practise / to / must / piano / the / I

_____ .

2 day / should / I / study / every

_____ .

3 learn / Mark / does / to/ have / English / not

_____ .

4 for / must / not / lesson / he / late / his / be

_____ .

2 never / sometimes / usually / often / always

3 **Write sentences using adverbs of frequency.**

sometimes	never	often	always	usually

1 I _always tidy my room._

2 I _____ .

3 I _____ .

4 I _____ .

5 I _____ .

6 I _____ .

meet my friends
revise for a test
brush my teeth
tidy my room
do my homework
be on time
make my bed
wash my face
take notes in class

4 **What do you do? Read and complete.**

1 In summer, I usually _go to the beach with my family._____

2 At the weekend, I always _____ .

3 On Wednesday afternoons, I often _____ .

4 I never go _____ on Sundays.

5 Sometimes, I like to _____ in the morning.

6 I _____ eat chocolate and _____ .

7 I never eat _____ .

5 **Read. Then complete using the graph.**

I ¹ _usually get up_____ at seven o'clock.

I ² _____ at quarter to eight.

I ³ _____ at eight o'clock,

before leaving for school.

At home, I ⁴ _____ because

it's my brother who has to do it.

After dinner I ⁵ _____ .

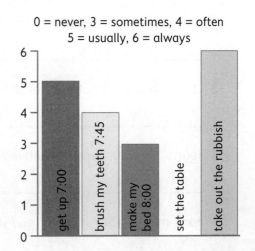

0 = never, 3 = sometimes, 4 = often
5 = usually, 6 = always

6 **Read. Then match.**

1 I'm going to the cinema

   a to go for a swim.

   b to see Toy Story 3.

   c to play basketball.

2 I've got a ticket

   a to play football.

   b to go shopping.

   c to go to the concert.

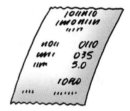

3 He's going to the stadium

   a to watch a film.

   b to see a football match.

   c to run a race.

4 They're taking the train

   a to brush their teeth.

   b to be film stars.

   c to get to work.

5 She's got her swimsuit

   a to go swimming.

   b to ride a bike.

   c to go to the party.

7 **Read. Then complete.**

1 You revise to _____ .

2 You save money to _____ .

3 You went to the supermarket to _____ .

4 Your tongue helps you to _____ .

8 **Read. Then complete.**

should shouldn't must always should never should shouldn't

When you go shopping in a market you ¹_____**should**_____ always be careful.

You ²_____ always carry your bag in front of you. ³_____ open

your purse or wallet in the street to look for money. You ⁴_____ try to

look behind you when you are walking and you ⁵_____ stop to look

at a map. ⁶_____ wear a money belt under your coat to hide your

money. Don't attract attention. You ⁷_____ wear expensive clothes

or jewellery. Markets are great places to go shopping but you ⁸_____

be careful!

9 **Look at the pictures. Then give advice. Use** *always.*

1

You should always _____.

2

_____.

3

_____.

4

_____.

Free time 3

What are you good at?

1 **Write sentences.**

1 _____ . (Tom / not good / catching)

2 _____ . (Sam / good / throwing)

3 _____ . (they / good / singing)

4 _____ . (we / not good / acting)

5 _____ ! (I / good / English)

2 **Write questions. Then answer for yourself.**

1    <u>Are you good at</u> _____ ? _____ .

2    _____ ? _____ .

3    _____ ? _____ .

4    _____ ? _____ .

3   What were you doing yesterday?

3 Read. Then complete.

At 5 o'clock yesterday, I ¹ <u>**was playing**</u> (play) on the computer. My little

brother ² _____ (kick) a ball in the garden. My sister ³ _____

(practise) the guitar and my big brother ⁴ _____ (read) a magazine. My

parents ⁵ _____ (chat) to some friends.

4 Order to make questions. Then answer for yourself.

1 seven / you / o'clock / doing / were / yesterday / what / at

_____ ?

I was _____ .

2 watching / a / you / DVD / were / yesterday / afternoon

_____ ?

_____ .

3 doing / were / your / what / friends / at / eight / o'clock

_____ ?

_____ .

4 your / volleyball / were / playing / friends

_____ ?

_____ .

5 were / school / to / Saturday / going / on / morning / they / 8:00 / at

_____ ?

_____ .

6 parents / were / playing chess / your / o'clock / at / nine

_____ ?

_____ .

5 **Look at the table. Then make sentences using *prefer*.**

1st choice	2nd choice
rollerblading	skateboarding
dancing	singing
playing football	playing volleyball
playing video games	going shopping
throwing	catching

1 <u>I prefer rollerblading to skateboarding.</u>

2 _____ .

3 _____ .

4 _____ .

5 _____ .

6 **Read. Then circle.**

1 I prefer *singing* / *sing* to dancing.

2 Dad prefers *cook* / *cooking* to cleaning.

3 I'd rather *watch* / *watching* TV than go out.

4 We'd rather *sing* / *singing* than dance.

5 They prefer *play* / *playing* video games to playing football.

7 **Read. Then complete.**

1 She is good at hitting. She would rather _____ (play) tennis than football.

2 He prefers _____ (trampoline) to _____ (play) cricket.

3 I'm lazy. I prefer _____ (play) video games to _____ (run) races.

4 After school I would rather _____ (meet) my friends than _____

(do) my homework!

8 **Look at the table. Then write questions and answers.**

Yesterday	Tom	Sara
9:00	sleeping	playing football
11:00	playing video games	meeting friends
14:00	having lunch	having lunch
15:00	climbing trees	rollerblading

1 <u>What was Tom doing at nine o'clock yesterday?</u>   (Tom / 9:00)

  <u>He was sleeping.</u>

2 _____ ? (Sara / 9:00)

  _____ .

3 _____ ? (Sara / 11:00)

  _____ .

4 _____ ? (Tom / 15:00)

  _____ .

5 _____ ? (Tom and Sara / 14:00)

  _____ .

9 **Read. Then circle.**

1 **Tom:** Are you good at *skateboard* / *skateboarding*?

2 **Sara:** Not really. I prefer rollerblading *to* / *than* skateboarding.

3 **Tom:** I'm not good *at* / *in* rollerblading. I'd rather *play* / *playing* video games

   than / *in* play sport!

4 **Sara:** I'm not good at *playing* / *play* video games.

Around the world

There isn't a ... / There aren't any ...

1 **Order to make sentences.**

1 there / any / in / aren't / Canada / crocodiles

_____ .

2 Greece / a / there / rainforest / isn't / in

_____ .

3 in / waterfall / is / a / there / England

_____ .

4 aren't / penguins / Spain / there / any / in

_____ .

5 Great / in / Brazil / Wall / there / a / isn't

_____ .

6 there / beautiful / Australia / are / beaches / some / in

_____ .

2 **Read. Then write questions and answers**

1 hippos / Poland ✘   **2** spiders / Australia ✔

3 mountains / Mexico ✔   **4** Great Wall / Japan ✘

5 waterfalls / Egypt ✔   **6** rainforest / Brazil ✔

1 <u>Are there any hippos in Poland?</u> _____   <u>No, there aren't.</u>

2 _____ ? _____ .

3 _____ ? _____ .

4 _____ ? _____ .

5 _____ ? _____ .

6 _____ ? _____ .

4 Is there a ...? / Are there any ...?

3 **Look at the picture. Then answer.**

1 Are there any volcanoes? __No, there aren't.__

2 Is there a dog in the sea? _____ .

3 Is there a monkey in the tree? _____ .

4 Are there any penguins? _____ .

5 Is there a boy throwing a ball? _____ .

4 **Read. Then write the answers.**

1 Is there a Sphinx in Egypt?   ✔ _____ .

2 Is the River Nile in Colombia?   ✘ _____ .

3 Are there any snowstorms in Greenland? ✔ _____ .

4 Is there a large ocean on Mars?   ✘ _____ .

5 Is there a rainforest in Spain?   ✔ _____ .

5 **Look. Then write questions.**

1 __Are there any lakes in Egypt?__

  __Yes, there are.__

2 __Is there ...__ _____ ?

  _____ .

3 _____ ?

  _____ .

4 _____ ?

  _____ .

5 _____ ?

  _____ .

6 _____ ?

  _____ .

6 **Complete the questions with *much* or *many*.**

1 How _**many**_ mountains are there in Poland?

2 How _____ sand is there in Egypt?

3 How _____ volcanoes are there on Mercury?

4 How _____ water is there on Mars?

5 How _____ rivers are there in Argentina?

6 How _____ lakes are there in your country?

7 **Read. Then circle.**

1 How many pyramids are there in Egypt?

   a A few.
   b A little.
   c Not much.

2 How many Italian islands are there?

   a A lot.
   b A little.
   c Not much.

3 How much of Australia is desert?

   a A lot.
   b A few.
   c Not many.

4 How many oceans are there on Earth?

   a A few.
   b Not much.
   c A little.

5 How much gravity is there on Mercury?

   a Not many.
   b A few.
   c A little.

6 How much land is there on Mars?

   a A few.
   b Not many.
   c A lot.

8 **Read. Then answer the questions. Use short answers.**

1 Is there a volcano in Italy?

Yes, there is. ✔

2 Are there any penguins in Argentina?

_____ ✔

3 Is there any water on Mars?

_____ ✗

4 Are there any mountains in London?

_____ ✗

5 Is there an ocean on Jupiter?

_____ ✔

6 Is there a statue in your school?

_____

9 **Read. Then circle.**

Do you need a holiday? How ¹*many / much* time have you got?

There are so ²*many / much* places to visit.

What about visiting Greece?

There ³*is / are* a lot of islands to visit.

Or you could stay in Athens, the capital city.

There ⁴*is / are* a lot of accommodation.

How ⁵*many / much* do you want to pay?

There are a lot of cheap hotels and ⁶*some / any* expensive hotels.

And the food! There ⁷*are / is* a lot of different food.

The seafood is delicious and there ⁸*is / are* a lot of very good fish restaurants.

And the beaches ... There are so ⁹*much / many* beautiful beaches.

You must come to Greece!

Shopping 5

How much is it?

1 **Order to make questions. Then answer.**

1 much / that / how / is / watch

_____ ?

_____ .

2 gloves / those / are / much / how

_____ ?

_____ .

3 bracelet / that / how / much / is

_____ ?

_____ .

4 those / sunglasses / are / how / much

_____ ?

_____ .

£30

£18

£49

£97

2 **Read. Then complete the dialogue.**

it	eighty-five	~~much~~	here	change
expensive	them	those	they	how	are

Sara: How ¹ **much** is that jacket?

Assistant: ²_____ is fifty pounds.

Sara: And, how much are ³_____ sunglasses?

Assistant: ⁴_____ are sixty-five pounds.

Sara: Oh dear! That's too ⁵_____ . Hmm, ⁶_____ much ⁷_____ those ?

Assistant: They're thirty-five pounds fifty.

Sara: Okay. I'll take ⁸_____ . And I'll take the jacket.

Assistant: That'll be ⁹_____ pounds fifty.

Sara: ¹⁰_____ is a hundred pounds.

Assistant: Thank you. Here is your ¹¹_____ : five and ten.

5 Whose jumper is this?

3 Read the answers. Then write the questions.

1 <u>Whose jumper is this?</u>   It's his jumper.

2 _____ ? They're Sue's trainers.

3 _____ ? It's my watch.

4 _____ ? They're William's books.

5 _____ ? They're Sara's glasses.

6 _____ ? It's Tom's tracksuit.

7 _____ ? It's Steph's bracelet.

8 _____ ? They're Maria's gloves.

4 Find the mistakes. Then correct.

1 This sandwich is <u>my</u>.   <u>This sandwich is mine.</u>

2 These umbrellas are your. _____ .

3 This ball is Tom. _____ .

4 These kittens are her. _____ .

5 This watch is him. _____ .

6 These trousers are your. _____ .

7 This hat is Sarah. _____ .

5 Read. Then circle.

1 These flowers are mine.   These are *mine* / *my* flowers.

2 This book is his.   This is *his* / *he* book.

3 Those chips are hers.   Those are *his* / *her* chips.

4 These clothes are ours.   These are *ours* / *our* clothes.

5 This is their picture.   The picture is *their* / *theirs*.

6 Those trousers are yours.   Those are *you* / *your* trousers.

7 That is her wallet.   That wallet is *her* / *hers*.

6 **Order to make questions. Then answer for yourself.**

1 to / what / going / today / are / after / you / do / school

_____ ?

_____ .

2 are / to / watch / evening / what / on / TV / this / you / going

_____ ?

_____ .

3 are / weekend / parents / going / your / to /at / the / what / do

_____ ?

_____ .

4 tomorrow / friends / are /going / do / what / your / to

_____ ?

_____ .

7 **Complete the dialogue. Use *will* /*won't*.**

Ben: I think it [1] **will rain**_____ (rain) tomorrow.

Jenny: No, it [2]_____ (not rain)! It [3]_____ (be)

hot and sunny!

Ben: Really? Then I think I [4]_____ (go) to the beach.

Jenny: Good idea. I [5]_____ (look for) my swimsuit.

(a bit later)

Jenny: Oh no! My swimsuit's full of holes! I think I

[6]_____ (have to) buy a new one.

Ben: Okay. We [7]_____ (go) shopping! The shops

[8]_____ (not be) busy today.

8 **Find the mistakes. Then correct.**

1 Look at the sky! It's going rain!

   Look at the sky! It's going to rain! _____

2 What are you going do at the weekend?

   _____ ?

3 I think I will to go to the film at six o'clock.

   _____ .

4 Me too! I going see the latest Superman film.

   _____ .

5 Really? Maybe I will to see you at the cinema!

   _____ !

9 **Read. Then circle.**

1

> We're going on holiday!
> I can't believe it! This afternoon we
> *are going to* / *will* pack our suitcases.
>
> Here are *our* / *ours* clothes. Is this
> skirt *you* / *yours*, Kate?

2

> No, it isn't *me* / *mine*.

3

> What about *these* / *this*
> trainers. Are they
> *you* / *yours*?

4

> No. I don't think so.

5

> This tracksuit is Johnny's. And
> these trousers are *he* / *his*, too.

6

> No, the trousers are
> *my* / *mine*. Do you
> like *it* / *them*?

Party time

They brought a present

1 **Read. Then complete the tables.**

Present	Past
make	**made**
	had
come	
	could
eat	

Present	Past
give	
bring	
	met
see	
	went

2 **Read. Then complete using the past tense.**

When I was seven, I ¹__could__ (can) play the piano a little. I ²_____ (have) a really

good piano teacher. She ³_____ (be) very kind and ⁴_____ (help) me to learn a

lot. I ⁵_____ (play) in front of my school. That ⁶_____ (be) great.

I ⁷_____ (be) really excited. All my family ⁸_____ (come) to watch me.

Then my class ⁹_____ (sing) two of my favourite songs. We ¹⁰_____ (be)

really happy.

Now, I'm eight. Last term, I ¹¹_____ (start) to learn the guitar. I love playing

the guitar. It's quite difficult but I ¹²_____ (practise) everyday for the first month.

And I ¹³_____ (take) my guitar on holiday with me. Every evening, my family and

friends ¹⁴_____ (sing) songs and I ¹⁵_____ (play) the guitar. I think we

¹⁶_____ (make) a lot of noise!

6 Where did you go?

3 Write sentences.

1 I / eat / a pizza ✗ // eat / a hamburger ✔ <u>I didn't eat a pizza, I ate a hamburger.</u>

2 he / come / today ✗ // come / yesterday ✔ _____ .

3 we / go / Spain ✗ // go / Argentina ✔ _____ .

4 she / meet / Tom ✗ // meet / me ✔ _____ .

5 they / see / giraffe ✗ // see / hippo ✔ _____ .

6 she / buy / a present ✗ // buy / a cake ✔ _____ .

4 Order to make questions. Then answer for yourself.

1 you / year / holiday / where / on / did / go / last

_____ ?

_____ .

2 go / did / with / you / who

_____ ?

_____ .

3 did / who / meet / you

_____ ?

_____ .

4 do / did / what / you

_____ ?

_____ .

5 you / what / see / did

_____ ?

_____ .

6 type / of / did / what / food / eat / you

_____ ?

_____ .

5 Read Linda's list. Then write sentences using *must* or *have to*.

> **To do:**
> ✔ call Sara
> finish my story
> do my homework
> write to granny
> tidy my room
> practise the piano

1 I must call Sara. _____

2 _____ .

3 _____ .

4 _____ .

5 _____ .

6 _____ .

6 Find the mistakes. Then correct.

1 I have walk to school every day.

   I have to walk to school every day. _____

2 I have buy a present for Grandad.

   _____ .

3 I must finishing my homework.

   _____ .

4 I have meeting Sara after school.

   _____ .

5 My parents say I must to go to bed before nine o'clock.

   _____ .

6 Revision

7 Order to make sentences.

1 friends / have / to / meet / Friday / on / I / my

_____ .

2 weekend / last / did / go / you / the / cinema / to

_____ ?

3 grandad / must / I / write / my / to

_____ .

4 meet / you / party / did / who / the /at

_____ ?

5 when / see / film / the / did / you

_____ ?

6 should / your / at / meet / friends / you / five o'clock

_____ .

8 Read. Then rewrite in the opposite form.

1 The film *was* very interesting.

The film wasn't very interesting. _____

2 I *could play* the violin last year.

_____ .

3 He *didn't watch* TV yesterday evening.

_____ .

4 My friends *came* to my house yesterday.

_____ .

5 We *didn't meet* Tom and Sara after school.

_____ .

6 She *made* a cake for his birthday yesterday afternoon.

_____ .

1 Order to make questions. Then answer for yourself.

1 any / homework / was / yesterday / Maths / there

_____ ?

_____ .

2 computers / class / were / in / there / any / yesterday

_____ ?

_____ .

3 interesting / your / was / class / last

_____ ?

_____ .

4 to / school / you / late / were

_____ ?

_____ .

2 Write questions and answers.

1 **Was the film funny?**   **No, it wasn't.** ✗
   (film / funny)

2 _____ ? _____ . ✔
   (poem / boring)

3 _____ ? _____ . ✗
   (school lessons / difficult)

4 _____ ? _____ . ✗
   (homework / easy)

5 _____ ? _____ . ✔
   (book / interesting)

7 Did you have Maths on Friday?

3 Read. Then match.

1 Did you go to bed early last night?

2 Did you read the Harry Potter books in English?

3 Did you go to school last week?

4 Did you eat all the vegetables?

5 Did you see the Batman film?

a No, I didn't. I was ill.

b No, I didn't. I ate the meat.

c Yes, I did. I went to bed at 7 o'clock.

d No, I didn't. They're too long!

e No, we didn't. We saw Superman.

4 Read the answers. Then write the questions.

1 <u>Did you go to England last year ?</u>

No, I didn't. I went to Italy.

2 _____ ?

No, I didn't. But I saw lots of frogs and small lizards.

3 _____ ?

No, I didn't. I stayed at home and read a comic.

4 _____ ?

No, I didn't. I studied English.

5 Order to make questions.

1 the / scary / film / did / have / alien / an

_____ ?

2 Maths / Maddy / did / homework / Monday / on / have

_____ ?

3 Drama / were / interesting / lessons / Monday / last / your

_____ ?

4 there / Science / last / in / was / exciting / class / anything / your

_____ ?

6 **Read. Then match.**

1 Have you eaten ...

2 Have you used ...

3 Have you written ...

4 Have you watched ...

5 Have you sung ...

6 Have you finished ...

a that book?

b a film in 3D?

c the email to your friend?

d the glue?

e fish and chips?

f karaoke?

7 **Write questions and answers using the present perfect.**

1 (you / paint / picture)

   Have you drawn the picture?

   Yes, I have. ✔

2 (your friends / play / a football match)

   _____ ?

   _____ ✘

3 (you / revise / Maths / for / your / exam)

   _____ ?

   _____ ✔

4 (Tom / choose / a title / for / his / new book)

   _____ ?

   _____ ✘

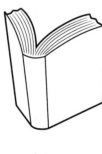

5 (Sara / be / the / museum /at)

   _____ ?

   _____ ✔

8 **Read. Then answer the questions.**

1 Did you go to the cinema last week? _____No, I didn't._____ ✗

2 Was it your birthday yesterday? _____ . ✔

3 Were there any children at school yesterday? _____ . ✗

4 Was there any homework yesterday? _____ . ✔

5 Did they sing good songs? _____ . ✗

6 Were there any good presents at the party? _____ . ✔

9 **Read. Then complete.**

¹**Have you been** (you be) to Wales? It's amazing. I have ²_____ (be) there 5 times! I ³_____ (go) again last month with my family.

When I first ⁴_____ (go) I ⁵_____ (not know) they speak a different language! I ⁶_____ (not hear) much English spoken at all. I ⁷_____ (try) to say some of the words. But it ⁸_____ (be) impossible! Some words ⁹_____ (not have) a vowel!

During our last 3 visits we ¹⁰_____ (stay) in a lot of small towns in the north of the country. We ¹¹_____ (sleep) in hotels, apartments and even in tents on a campsite. The last time we ¹²_____ (go camping) it rained everyday so finally mum said that we ¹³_____ (have to) find a hotel! We ¹⁴_____ (not be) very surprised! We ¹⁵_____ (have) our waterproof coats and boots !It ¹⁶_____ (rain) a lot in Wales!

When we ¹⁷_____ (get) home the first thing I ¹⁸_____ (want) to do was to have a warm bath! If you ¹⁹_____ (not be) to Wales you should go, but don't forget your umbrella!

10 **Read. Then complete using the present perfect.**

1 **Have** you _____ (finish) your lunch?

2 _____ they _____ (visit) Paris?

3 _____ she _____ (help) her mum?

4 _____ he _____ (study) English?

All about us

Is he from Italy?

1 Read. Then write.

1 I come from Colombia. <u>I'm Colombian.</u>

2 We come from China. _____ .

3 They come from Spain. _____ .

4 He comes from Canada. _____ .

5 She comes from Turkey. _____ .

2 Read. Then complete.

1 Hi there! I'm Jaime. I'm from Spain. I'm _____ . These are my friends.

2 Paula is from Thailand. She's _____ .

3 Johnny is from Brazil. He's _____ .

4 Monika and Anna are from _____ . They are Polish.

5 And Simon is from _____ . He's British.

3 Find the conversation. Then write.

where →	are	Yes	they	Mexican	are
from	you	?	are	and	you
?	I'm	Argentina	Argentinian	they	so
Mexico	from	from	.	are	are
.	Are	they	.	Argentinian	.

A: _____

B: _____

A: _____

B: _____

A: _____

8   A friend who ... / A film that ...

4 Read. Then write sentences.

1 She is a girl from school. She helped me carry my suitcase.

<u>She is the girl from school who helped me carry my suitcase.</u>

2 He is a teacher. He teaches P.E.

_____ .

3 Karen is my friend. She beat me in the tennis match!

_____ .

4 They are film stars. They were in the park.

_____ .

5 They are Australians. They taught me how to surf.

_____ .

5 Look at the flags and complete. Then write sentences using *who* or *that*.

1 This is a popular ball game. It comes from <u>Spain.</u>

<u>This is a popular ball game that comes from Spain.</u>

2 She's an _____ singer. She sings all over the world.

_____ .

3 This is a car. It is made in _____ .

_____ .

4 He's a _____ sailor. He tried to sail across the Atlantic Ocean.

_____ .

5 These are computers. They were made in _____ .

_____ .

6 He's a famous astronaut. He's from _____ .

_____ .

6 **Read. Then write *in, on* or *at*.**

¹_____ spring, when I have to go to school, I get up ²_____ 8 o'clock ³_____

the morning. It's usually very dark. I don't like getting up ⁴_____ the dark. ⁵_____ June,

when the days are longer and it's lighter ⁶_____ the morning, I get up ⁷_____ half past

six. ⁸_____ Thursdays I get up at 6 o'clock because I've got swimming lessons before school.

It feels like the middle of the night! During the school holidays, I always get up late! My mum calls

me for breakfast ⁹_____ 10 o'clock. ¹⁰_____ the morning, I go out on my bike. I stay out

with my friends until about five o'clock and then I go home for tea. I usually go to bed

¹¹_____ ten o'clock. I love school holidays!

7 **Read. Then write sentences.**

I go to bed		26th November.
Carnival is usually	in	Christmas Day.
My birthday is		February.
My aunt won the lottery	on	1970.
It's always cold		nine o'clock.
I get lots of presents	at	winter.

1 I go to bed at nine o'clock._____

2 _____ .

3 _____ .

4 _____ .

5 _____ .

6 _____ .

8 Read. Then circle.

1 This is the swimming pool *where* / *who* I go before school.

2 These are the friends *which* / *who* play with me.

3 Those are the presents *where* / *which* I got for my birthday.

4 That is the song *where* / *which* I've got to learn.

5 She is the aunt *which* / *who* takes me ice skating.

6 That is the place *which* / *where* I play volleyball.

9 Quiz! Read and write sentences using *who* or *which*. Then answer.

1 This is a city. It is the capital of Argentina.

? This is a city which is the capital of Argentina.

: It's Buenos Aires!

2 This is a special celebration. It's celebrated on the 25th of December.

? _____ .

: _____

3 This is an important person in England. She lives in Buckingham Palace.

? _____ .

: _____

4 This is a very big place. You watch your favourite football team there.

? _____ .

: _____

5 This is a famous festival. It's celebrated on the last day of October.

? _____ .

: _____